I0135466

Yoruba Culture
Proverbs Vol 1

Complied by Sisi Tosin and Illustrated by Tehan Jones

Yoruba Culture - Proverbs Vol 1
Compiled by Sisi Tosin

Published by DaReaders House

Illustrations by Tehran Jones

For Information contact:

DaReaders House
PO BOX 3794
Lisle, IL 60532

ISBN 978-0-9981590-0-3

Dedicated to all the "ọmọ karo ṣe o ji re" out there

Aṣọ àtàtà kìí gbayì nínú àpò

A beautiful clothe kept in a bag, can not appreciated.

Meaning

an sweurs and cusses
ause he lacks the
abulary to fully
ress himself

et your light shine; don't cover up your
ift

Ìwà rere lẹ̀sọ́ ènìyàn

Good character is what adorns a man.

Meaning

Good character is honorable and attractive.

Ẹni tó bá fẹ́ fò, gbọ́dọ̀ kọ́kọ́ sáré

Whoever wants to fly, must first run.

Meaning

Success don't just happen, it has to be prepared for.

Only a patient person can get to milk a lioness.

Onísùúrù ló ńfún wàrà kìnìún.

Meaning

With patience, exceptional outcome is achievable.

HOME
SWEET
HOME

*Òde ò ní dùn kí onílé
má re'lé.*

An outing can't be so nice that one won't return home.

Meaning

No matter where you go, home is where the heart is.

Òkò tí a bá
bínú jù kìí
pẹyẹ

A stone thrown at a bird in anger can't kill the bird.

Meaning

Actions taken in anger seldom achieve desired results

A dog can't be so vicious as to be able to watch over two houses.

Ajá kì í rorò títí kí ó ṣọ́ ojú'lé méjì.

Meaning

5060

here is a limit to what
ny one person can do;
here is power in numbers.

Ọjọ́ ti ọmọdé nàró kọ ni í rìn.

It's not the day a baby stands up for the first time that he (or she) walks.

Meaning

Be patient; good things take time.

Mòjà mòsá ni ti akínkanjú; akínkanjú tó bá mòó jà tí ò mòó sá, á b'ógun lọ.

A warrior must know when to fight and when to run; a warrior who know when to fight but not when to run wi perish in battle.

Meaning

Good to know when to pursue and when to quit.

A kì í wo ago aláago șișé.

Don't carry out your duties using someone else's watch.

Meaning

Don't compare yourself with anyone

www.ingramcontent.com/pod-product-compliance
Lightning Source LLC
Chambersburg PA
CBHW042351030426

42336CB00025B/3441